STONE BLESSINGS

STONE BLESSINGS

Meditations

ROBERT WALSH

SKINNER HOUSE BOOKS

BOSTON

Printed in the United States

Cover and text design by Suzanne Morgan
Cover art, *Beach Rocks,* by Patricia Frevert

ISBN 1-55896-560-2
978-1-55896-560-7

12 11 10
6 5 4 3 2 1

Library of Congress Cataloging-in-Publication Data

Walsh, Robert R., 1937-
  Stone blessings : meditations / Robert Walsh.
       p. cm.
  ISBN-13: 978-1-55896-560-7 (pbk. : alk. paper)
  ISBN-10: 1-55896-560-2 (pbk. : alk. paper)   1. Meditations.
2. Unitarian Universalist Association—Prayers and devotions. I. Title.
  BX9855.W35 2010
  242'.809132—dc22
                                   2009035652

I dedicate this book to:

Emma

Samantha

Rosalee

Caroline

Porter

and

Emmett

CONTENTS

In the Present	1
In the Soup	3
Like Home	4
Tears	6
New England Autumn	8
Interdependence	9
The Unproven God	10
Good Company	12
The Dark Llama	14
An Icon	16
Winter	18
Passing Through	19
Strutting	20
Alive Again	21
Meditation While Picking Up Litter Along Route 3A	22
At the Liberal Barber Shop	24
Morning Prayer	26
Early Easter	27

My Secret Ritual   28

Compost Story   30

Home Run   31

A Shoulder to Lean On   32

A Billion Voices Silenced   34

Glad to See You   36

Feeding and Being Fed   38

Songs I Sang   40

Abundance   42

Tucked In   44

Let Me Tell You About My Granddaughter   46

On Buying a Cemetery Plot   48

A Gray Whale and Her Calf in the
Laguna San Ignacio   50

Unitarian Universalist Meditation Manuals   54

IN THE PRESENT

On a sunny day, I walked alone in a broad valley in Nepal, through an old forest with vines and moss and flowering trees and intermittent vistas of the snow-covered Himalayas. I came upon a clearing in the woods, and saw there a holy man—a monk in an orange robe, head shaved, back bent with age—chopping wood.

I had conflicting impulses. I wanted to ask him questions. What was his name? Where did he live? What was his life like? I wanted his blessing, and I wanted to give him mine. And I wanted to pass by invisibly, noiselessly, doing nothing that would disturb him.

Instead, I took out my camera and took a picture of him. I tried to be as discreet as possible about it; I waited until he was not looking in my direction. I don't know whether he heard the sound. Then I put the camera away and moved on down the trail.

I took the picture because I wanted to hold on to that moment, because I wanted to tell you the story. Now I have a small, still, two-dimensional memento of that moment. We can look at it. It will last for a while. The actual moment completely surrounded me. It had sounds and smells and movement, and it was only real for a moment. Now it's gone, and it will never happen again.

I moved through that experience with my attention alternating between the present moment and a future time, when I would be back home, telling the story. It's what preachers call *homiletic consciousness*, which means going through life thinking, *Can I use this in a sermon?* But it's not just preachers who do it. I imagine a painter would do the same. Or a poet. Or a novelist, teacher, composer, or storyteller—anyone who uses the experiences of life in order to give something to someone else.

But the more we stay in the future, thinking about telling the story, the less we are open to the power of the experience itself. The more we put a frame around the picture, the more it becomes only a picture and not a real event. Instead of living life each day, we are busy getting ready for life.

Yet if it were not for storytellers and photographers, I would never have gone to Nepal.

So I will try to find a balance between being fully in the moment and being present to the whole of life—past, present, and future, here and there. That I may live this day today, and also tell the story tomorrow.

IN THE SOUP

My dictionary says the word *minister* is etymologically related to the word *minestrone*. I am not making this up. They are both derived from a Latin root that means *to serve*.

The image of ministry as minestrone is particularly apt for the ministry churchpeople do all together that makes us a ministering congregation. Each bean, each vegetable, each unit of macaroni or pinch of spice gives not only its substance to the soup but also its spirit, its texture and color, its flavor and aroma. Each person offers a unique set of gifts, and if we do our job of organizing well, each gift will be creatively matched with a need—so that the whole becomes a warm, nourishing, life-giving religious community.

All who serve the church and the principles and values we hold dear are ministers. If you are doing part of that work, you are doing ministry, no matter how unlikely it may seem. You are in the soup—the minestrone of ministry!

LIKE HOME

On the outskirts of Tucson, I walked into the Sonora Desert, where the thirty-foot-tall saguaro cactuses grow.

Every living organism there, plant or animal, seemed poised and ready to injure me. My companion said, "Yes, everything here will stick you or sting you or bite you." The trees had thorns. The bushes had stickers, and the cactuses had long, hard fearsome needles. One of them, called the barrel cactus, had needles, I swear, that were shaped like fishhooks, and felt as strong and as hard as fishhooks. I couldn't help but imagine tripping over something and falling onto one of those cactuses, and then it would be all over. I'd just be helplessly impaled on this giant plant. And I haven't even mentioned the coral snakes, the scorpions, and the venomous Gila monster.

I concluded that the Sonora Desert, though beautiful, even irresistible, is a hostile place. It doesn't want me there.

The world is, in part, the Sonora Desert. The world has a merciless burning sun, and thorns, and fishhook needles, and teeth, and venom. The world is, in part, hostile to us. We have learned that.

I returned home safely from my stay near the desert, and soon thereafter was permitted to babysit my seven-month-old granddaughter. Her parents trusted me enough to leave her in my care for several hours. My responsibility as sitter-grandfather is to make a safe place for her, a place of comfort and security, where she is protected for a while from the venom and thorns and hostility. A place where she is wanted. A place that is home.

For the world is also like that. There are forces that protect us from danger, that shield us from fire, and keep away the monsters. They are not invincible forces. They do not always work. But do not doubt that they are real. They include the power of love, justice, and mercy.

We are alive, and so we have been wounded by this world. And we will be wounded again. But we are alive and we have been loved; we have received kindness and known justice. May we trust that with faithful companions we can give our goodness to the world, and transform it. There will be healing, and there will be wholeness, and there will be beauty. And the world may become a little bit more like home for everyone.

TEARS

Sometimes tears come to my eyes.
Is it about the war?
Is it from getting older?
Or is it just autumn?

I'm self-conscious about it,
afraid people will think I'm grieving,
or that I'm a sentimental fool.
I guess they'd be right if they thought those things.

It happened when I had lunch with a friend I
hadn't seen in a long time.
It happened when I saw a bright orange maple tree
outside my office window.
It happened when I saw a bride, whom I have known
since she was six, kiss the groom.
It happened when one of my granddaughters
held out her arms to me.

It happened when I heard a song about a lost dream.
It happened when I recalled a promise I had broken,
and a thank-you I had not spoken.
It happened when I thought of a friend
who died in autumn.
It's happening now, as I write these words.

I wipe the tears away
and go on as if everything was normal.

But it's not normal, it's *intense*, full of joy and sorrow,
and the joy and the sorrow are together
in the same moments.

This is the life, and the world, I have been given
for this short time, this blink of an eye.

Thank you.

NEW ENGLAND AUTUMN

Why are we treated to this colorful show every year?

I am not aware of any survival value for the trees in their going through this bright showing-off phase. It makes no difference to the leaves—they are soon mulch, every red and yellow one of them.

In northern New England, a large tourist industry thrives on the human enjoyment of the fall colors. Sentient beings travel in machines to see decaying vegetable matter. Is this part of the Grand Design? Does it have survival value for us?

It is a mystery. After all the botanical analysis and theological speculation we are still left with the red and yellow leaves as a gift. There is no card to say who sent the gift, or why. Just the trees and the leaves and the chill air. It will be there for a while, and then it will change into something else. We can't store it up.

INTERDEPENDENCE

"Neither is it he that planteth nor he that watereth, but God that giveth the increase," said Paul. But the Vermont farmer said of his orderly spread, "You should have seen it when God was taking care of it all alone!"

The human and the divine depend on each other.

At the core of our prayers of gratitude are two spiritual transactions: an acknowledgment of our dependence on the mystery of creation, and an acceptance of responsibility to do our share of the creative work.

We are deeply connected to the fruitful earth, and we are called to its service.

THE UNPROVEN GOD

There's an Oxford philosophy professor who says he has determined by sheer logic and mathematics that God probably exists. While Dr. Richard Swinburne says he is not 100-percent sure about this, he claims to have demonstrated through probability theory and complex mathematical formulas that God's existence is more likely to be true than not.

The God he is trying to prove is a familiar one, and in some respects reassuring. This God is a person, and "he" loves beauty, goodness, freedom, order, morality, and human beings. Haven't we always hoped that God would turn out to be like the good side of us, only more powerful?

It seems bold of me to say this about a professor at Oxford, but I'm willing to state with confidence that Dr. Swinburne's calculations are pure hokum, complete balderdash. He thinks God is a problem to be solved. He doesn't get it that God is a mystery, and is always and forever beyond every mortal attempt to figure God out and settle God once and for all.

God cannot be proven nor disproved. If you can prove it, then it's not God; it's something less than God.

Live in the world. Experience its joys and its pain. Try to find the path through it that is right for you.

Listen carefully to the voices around you, the voices within you, and the voices from the past. You may come to know that there is a mystery animating the Creation and you. A creating, sustaining, transforming mystery. Or you may not. If you do, you may choose to give it a name; you may call it God. Or you may not. But don't waste any of your precious time trying to prove it.

GOOD COMPANY

I had a car accident on a sunny Saturday on the crowded expressway heading into the city.

I was driving in the fast lane when something went wrong up ahead. My little car got sandwiched between a delivery van ahead of me and a big new pickup truck behind. I was fourth in a six-vehicle pileup.

When everything came to rest, I sat alone in a daze. I became aware of a pain in my chest. I imagined internal injuries, or a heart attack. Tears came to my eyes. I was afraid.

Help came. First the police, then ambulance technicians, who took me to an emergency room, then nurses and doctors. Word came that friends were on the way. Waves of relief washed over me as I surrendered myself into the care of competent helpers.

Propped up in the emergency room bed, I was momentarily alone in my cubicle. The tears came again, this time tears of gratitude. I was still afraid—the pain in my chest was still there, and I did not know what my injuries were or what losses I might suffer. But now everything was different, for I was no longer alone.

Here's the best part: I was not alone even when I thought I was, out there in my crumpled car.

What ultimately keeps us company is a spirit that is present in caring people, a spirit of healing and wholeness and love. It is the spirit of Creation and it has many names. Caring people are the most wonderful and precious agents of that spirit, but I have come to believe that it is present even when caring people are not nearby.

Even in solitude, we are in good company. We are connected to the interdependent web of all being, and to the source of being beyond it. This connection is never far away. It is always accessible.

The problem is, we forget. That is why I was so afraid: I had forgotten. The caring people reminded me.

In times to come, may we remember and be grateful. When chaos breaks through the orderly background and sends life off in an unexpected and unwanted direction, may we remember and be grateful that we are not alone. And may each caring one of us be a reminder to others of our common gift of the good company of the spirit.

THE DARK LLAMA

One June night, while people in the southern hemisphere prepared for their winter solstice, I stood in a campground high in the Andes and looked at the sky. The Milky Way ran right over our heads in brilliant clarity.

Our guide pointed to formations in the bright band of light, and I realized that most of the patterns he pointed out were not patterns of stars but patterns made by the absence of stars. They were black areas within the thick bright stream of the Milky Way. It looked as though there were no stars there, but we were actually looking at dark nebulae that blocked out the light of the stars behind them. We were standing in the shadow of the nebulae.

The biggest dark area is a nebula that modern astronomers call the Coalsack. The Incas saw in it the shape of a llama. Nearby is a smaller dark patch they said is her baby. The dark nebula is pierced by two bright stars that they said form the big llama's eyes. The Incas told a story about the Great Llama, that as her head dips toward the horizon at the solstice, she is bending down to drink from the ocean. Her drinking prevents the floods that would otherwise come; and the water she drinks flows through the Milky Way and becomes nourishing rain.

The story of the Great Llama is a story of Creative Spirit revealed in darkness, not light. To the Inca observer, the starlight was the background, the foil. The darkness was the foreground.

It is a good story for our season of long nights in the Northern Hemisphere. It reverses our usual focus on the sunlight, the bright star, the candle flame. It invites us to allow the light to be the background and center our attention on the creative darkness. We may meditate upon the darkness of the blessed night that brings rest and healing; the darkness under the surface of the soil, where the fertile seed begins to grow; the darkness of the mother's womb. The old story of creation begins in the dark. All life begins in the dark.

AN ICON

On Monday morning, I got a call from a woman I did not know who wanted to arrange a memorial service for a friend. I asked why she was calling our church. She said she understood that Unitarian Universalist churches tended not to have a lot of religious symbols. She said, "You don't have a lot of *icons* in your church, do you?" I told her there were very few traditional religious symbols in our sanctuary. Then I remembered something.

There had been a Sunday afternoon family concert in the sanctuary. Helium balloons decorated the event. Some of the balloons slipped out of small hands and ascended to the high ceiling. By Monday morning, they had all come down again, except for one. It was one of those high-tech balloons that lasts a very long time. It sat on the ceiling right above the pulpit, in the shape of a round pillow. And on it was a big yellow smiley face.

Some people, if they saw this smiley face looking down upon our pulpit, might consider it an icon that confirms their worst suspicions of Unitarian Universalism. See, they would say, UUism is a religion of cockeyed optimism. They believe in "the progress of mankind onward and upward forever." They believe in a God who says, "Have a nice day."

It's true that, many years ago, Unitarians used to repeat that platitude about progressing onward and upward, but we've learned some things from the past century. Few of us today would proclaim the inevitability of progress. We do proclaim the persistence of the possibility of goodness. We don't expect to live happily ever after, and sometimes God seems to turn a fearsome face in our direction. But we do believe that as long as there is life, there is the possibility of justice, mercy, and love. There is the possibility of meaning.

P.S. The smiley face slowly descended, and was removed before the date of the memorial service.

WINTER

The tree has bared itself to my view.
Its limbs and branches,
its hidden complexity,
exposed.

So this is the framework that holds the thick leaves.
So many leaves as to block the sun,
the lost sun,
the sunken sun.

Now only the spindly thin wood
casts its shadow on the earth.

Not for me this display of basics,
of skeletal function,
of inner structure and meaning.

Today I seek insulation,
refuge,
boundaries.

I bundle, wrap, cover.

PASSING THROUGH

O Spirit that creates us, sustains us, transforms us, and judges us, may your many names be hallowed.

May there come a world that sings with your justice and mercy, your beauty and truth, and may we be your faithful partners in creation to bring that world about.

Accept us in our brokenness, even as we would accept our mortal sisters and brothers, parents and children, spouses and partners, neighbors, and enemies.

Tempt us with life. Try us with growth and change and loss. But help us at last to find the path, through temptations and trials, to wholeness.

For we are but passing through this world. Yours is the Creation, and the power, and the glory.

STRUTTING

On Monday morning, after the Super Bowl, a pundit spoke disapprovingly of the way players act when they score a touchdown—the way they strut and call attention to themselves in a gloating manner, and milk the crowd for applause. The commentator took this to be an excess of pride and possibly a lack of respect for the competitors who were not quite fast enough, strong enough, or rough enough that time. And, he speculated, it might also enhance the player's marketability for product endorsements.

It can be spiritually healthy to take pleasure in doing something well, and to let others know of that pleasure. It is not so healthy to claim all the credit for oneself. No one has ever won a game or accomplished any good thing without a lot of help. It is not so healthy to assign lesser worth to others because they have not done what you did. And yet, it is obvious that many of us enjoy watching people show off.

I confess that I have sometimes had a guilty fantasy in which I preach a *really good* sermon. I toss my manuscript aside and come prancing down out of the pulpit. The organ begins to play "The Macarena" and I do a little dance. Members of the congregation pick me up and carry me into coffee hour chanting, "Rob-*bie*! Rob-*bie*!" Later the phone rings; someone wants me to endorse a line of ecclesiastical garments.

ALIVE AGAIN

One of my favorite hymns is the one that begins, "O Life, that maketh all things new." I believe in a universe in which there is continual creation, not one that is winding down after an initial burst of creativity. I believe there is a newness, a birth in each moment of a life, and also a death. We are constantly dying and being reborn to new life.

One day, I was driving on the highway into the city and saw potholes in the pavement, trash and litter in the median strip, and huge tacky billboards and junky industrial buildings beside the road, and there were rude drivers cutting in front of me. I felt surrounded by images of ugliness, decay, and entropy—all of it the work of human hands.

Then there came on the radio a lovely song. It was Mel Tormé singing "A Nightingale Sang in Berkeley Square." I remembered then that creation is ongoing, that all things are being made new. I felt alive again. I smiled, and let go of some of the tension in my body, and forgave the litterers and rude drivers.

I don't mean to suggest that the heavenly choir is going to sound like Mel Tormé—though that's not a bad idea—but that on that day, this beautiful song mediated eternity for me. It was the human-made work of art that allowed my spirit to soar.

MEDITATION WHILE PICKING UP LITTER
ALONG ROUTE 3A

I'm doing good.
I'm looking good.
I'm cleaning up the world, doing God's work, setting
    a good example.
I'm angry at the people who tossed this trash from
    their car windows.
It lies in woods, in grass, among wildflowers, on the
    gravel beside the road.
I feel violated.
I call them names. I imagine delicious punishments.
I forgive them.
They are inherently worthy, they are my kin.
I concentrate on their worthiness, that my forgive-
    ness will not slip away.
I'm a good person, to forgive them.
I'm setting a good example.
There are worse things in the world than tossing
    trash along the road.
There is oppression, injustice, war.
Children die of pestilence, hunger, neglect.
The oppression, in this moment, is abstract.
The trash is present and real.
I never drop trash from my car window.
But I have done worse things.

Things not so visible.
Picking up this litter will not bring my life
   into balance.
On the scale of evil this trash is trivial.
But I'm still angry about it.
And I'm doing good.

AT THE LIBERAL BARBER SHOP

I've heard about a beauty parlor where all the liberal customers made their appointments for Fridays, so they could talk about politics, religion, sex, and other topics without fear of hostile reactions. It reminded me of being young in the South in the early 1960s, when I had a recurring fantasy of the Liberal Barber Shop.

At Brooks' Barber Shop in my home town, when conversation moved beyond the local high school football and basketball teams, it tended to be about segregation and states' rights, and the possibility of dropping the bomb on the Russians. There was never a dissenting voice. Waiting my turn, I would bury my nose in an old *Saturday Evening Post*, keep my mouth shut, and imagine what Brooks might do to my hair if he suspected that I favored school desegregation or nuclear disarmament.

It wouldn't be like this at the Liberal Barber Shop. It's not that the barber and his customers would have "liberal" views on everything. They would *be* liberal. They would express their disagreements (about politics, religion, sex, etc.) respectfully, and treat each other with civility. Though they might believe passionately, they would speak with the understanding that they might be wrong. The customer would feel so safe at the Liberal Barber

Shop that he could speak freely about abortion, free trade, the Iraq war, or same-sex marriage—even as the keen edge of the straight razor moved across his sideburns.

Maybe it's just a dream. People are people. And yet we are capable of overcoming our destructive impulses. We can build institutions that hold up respect and dignity, peace and reconciliation—institutions that keep calling on us, with all our brokenness, to live up to those values. I think we can even build a world like that, a little bit at a time.

MORNING PRAYER

Each morning I thank you
as I take down another day from the shelf,
the shelf so high I can't see how many are left.

Each morning I tell you
that I can use some help with this day.

I want to dive.
I want to go beneath the flotsam and foam
and easy pleasures
and comfortable dull habits
into the deeper currents that I know are there.

I keep bobbing to the surface.

Shallow or deep,
my actions this day
will be my offering to you.

EARLY EASTER

love is the voice under all silences,
the hope which has no opposite in fear
—E.E. CUMMINGS

Easter arrives in New England while spring is still mostly a promise. If there is anything we can trust, surely we can trust the Earth, in partnership with the sun, to put new leaves on the trees, to coax blossoms from the forsythia. Meanwhile, I watch through the window on a gray chilly day for the warming and the brightening to come.

Easter invites us to trust in something more amazing even than the coming of spring. Can we trust this: that love is more durable than life? Can we believe that love casts out fear? Can we have faith that love is the voice under all silences?

I trust, and I mistrust. From the quiet center of my self, I hear a trusting of love, a faith that the story about love is true. On the noisy surface of my life, I hedge my bets. I collect things, join organizations, and take out insurance, hoping to be saved.

That's why I need Easter. That's why we keep this celebration. It is because we need to hear the old story about love. We need to be reminded about the voice under all silences.

MY SECRET RITUAL

I'm going to tell you a secret. When I was a full-time minister, I used to have a small ritual that I would perform before going out to the sanctuary to lead worship and preach, or to perform some rite of passage. I would go into my office and close the door, reach into the closet for my robe, put the robe on with a flourish, and say, "This looks like a job for Clergy-Man!"

I was invoking the spirit, not so much of Superman or any other super-hero, but of Clark Kent, the mild-mannered reporter—the shy, clumsy, self-doubting one who, by donning his special costume, could assume extraordinary powers.

Now, my robe doesn't empower *this* shy, clumsy, self-doubting one to leap tall buildings at a single bound, or to fly faster than a speeding bullet. But the role of ordained parish minister—of which my robe is a symbol—can empower one to do some extraordinary things that, I think, are even better.

I can help people find a path toward spiritual wholeness, toward integrity, love, and purpose. I can celebrate loving, faithful covenants between people in families and in the church. I can bring the healing spirit of the church and its tradition into the presence of the suffering and the dying. I can proclaim the truth of the inherent worth and dignity of every person. I can help carry forward a living religious community that covenants to walk together in freedom and responsibility. I can speak out for justice and peace. I can help feed the hungry and shelter the homeless.

Isn't that better than being able to fly?

But here's the best part: We can all do these things. We don't need to be ordained. It's not necessary to wear a robe or a stole—or a cape. We can all be ministers.

For persons who are called to professional ministry, ordination and its symbols are important. But there is a limit to what the professional leader can accomplish directly. To change the world, we need the ministry of everyone.

COMPOST STORY

At our house, I'm in charge of the compost.

We have a big jar-like container that sits on the kitchen counter, and we put things that we don't eat in there, like apple cores, orange peels, coffee grounds, egg shells, and leftovers that have been in the refrigerator too long. Every few days, I carry it outside to put the contents in a big box with a lid on it. The stuff stays in the box for a long time. Every once in a while, I stir it up with a pitchfork. Eventually, it becomes rich material I can mix into the garden soil to help things grow. Compost.

Just before Easter, I discovered something growing out of a hole at the bottom of the box. It was a beautiful flower, a hyacinth.

Somehow the bulb of this hyacinth got into our compost box, and lay there for a long time, through two or three cold winters. Every few days I piled some more garbage on top of it. Then this April, the little bulb somehow sensed that it was spring, and that the sun was shining nearby, and so out of this smelly compost it poked this beautiful blossom.

This hyacinth is a messenger of hope. It says, We may be small, and in this life we may get a lot of unpleasant stuff dumped on us. But we can overcome that, and dealing with that unpleasant stuff can even make us stronger and braver and wiser, and we can stand tall and proud in the sunshine and be beautiful.

HOME RUN

I hit a home run last Sunday!

It was in the church softball game. I didn't hit the ball all that far, but I was helped out by a series of "errors" by the other team as I ran around the bases.

I've never seen a softball game quite like this one. The players range in age from about four to about sixty-four. When the batter swings and misses three times in a row, the pitcher *continues to pitch until the batter hits one!* And when there are three outs, the batting team *remains at bat until each member of the team has had a turn!* And at the end of the day, though no one can remember how many runs there have been, it is announced that *the game was a tie!*

I'm sure there are folks who would view this with alarm. It doesn't teach us, they might say, about the world as it really is. The race goes to the swift. Winning, if not everything, is certainly the main thing.

Well, competition is a good thing in its place, and we do not lack for sporting events that teach us that. The First Parish softball game teaches something else. It points toward a world of cooperation, a world of respect and encouragement for people with varying abilities, in which every person brings a unique and valued gift to the common endeavor, in which there is joy and delight in play, without the need for winning or losing.

A SHOULDER TO LEAN ON

As I hiked down from a high mountain saddle above Dharamsala, a rain shower passed and the old stone path became slippery. I slipped and fell.

I hit my cheekbone on a rock and cut my thumb on the sharp edge of another rock. It hurt, and I was afraid. Afraid that I might have broken something; afraid that I might get some awful infection from the wound. My climbing companion came quickly and sat with me until I got over the shock and was able to stand.

We started down the trail again. I discovered that my tired knees were even more rubbery than before my fall, and I was afraid of falling again. I knew I needed some help. I said, "May I lean on you as we walk?" He said, "Of course." I put my hand on his shoulder and leaned on him as we walked the rest of the way back to the town.

It was not an easy thing to ask for help. I was taking pride in my ability to get up and down that mountain on my own two feet. My self-reliance had usually worked for me, but in that moment I surrendered it. And my companion gave me his shoulder to lean on. Just like it says in all those songs.

If, one day, you should stumble along life's path and injure yourself—and you may be sure that you will—listen for the rhythms of a deeper support than just what you hear from within.

There are currents, tides, rhythms of creativity, often expressed through the kindness of others, that can hold us up, heal our spiritual wounds, and move us along toward Dharamsala, or wherever we are called to go.

A BILLION VOICES SILENCED

In 1989, there arose in China a passionate, peaceful mass movement, led by students demanding freedom and democracy. The government sent the People's Liberation Army to crush the rebellion. Troops fired into crowds, killing many unarmed people.

Twenty years later, the people in China who remember know they must not speak of it. Young people do not hear of it in their history classes.

It has been said that the genie of liberty, once released, cannot be put back in the bottle; that the people will rise again. Perhaps it is true. But if so, it is a long-term truth. We know from history that tyrannical governments can successfully destroy liberty for long periods, longer than the lifetimes of many people.

I believe there is a creative spirit at work everywhere in the world, and that it is powerful and moves human affairs toward liberation, justice, and peace. But I am not convinced it is an omnipotent force. It seems possible to me that God will lose. At least in the short run.

It is important to remember that human beings are the agents of the spirit. The peaceful movement of the students in Beijing was an incarnation of the spirit. Each of us chooses the degree to which we express that spirit in our lives.

Freedom is perishable; cruelty and the lust for power are persistent aspects of our nature. Let each of us do what we can in our part of the Creation to move it toward our vision of the world that can be.

GLAD TO SEE YOU

The drivers on the island of Dominica blow their horns a lot. I was there for a week and drove a rented car over truly terrible roads, and on the left side too. The roads are narrow mountain roads with no center lines, no speed limits, and lots of blind curves.

The car rental guy explained. When they blow their horns, they may be warning whoever or whatever might be around the corner, but more often it's in the nature of a greeting—they are just glad to see you. I think maybe they're also glad to be alive, to have a destination ahead, and to have all four wheels on the narrow road, passing through the beauty of the rain forest and the misty mountains.

Soon I got into the spirit of it and began to give a little honk when I met another car. Eventually, I learned to wave at the other driver as I steered with one hand.

At first, I was suspicious of the friendliness of the Dominicans. I assumed they wanted something from me. I assumed they wanted to sell me something, or ask for a handout. Some of them did. But most were just, as the man said, glad to see me. After a while, I began to trust their essential goodwill and relax.

The "kingdom of God" is a mysterious idea to me. I'm not sure what it means. But if it came to be, I imagine as one of its characteristics that people would always be glad to see each other. They would react to the presence of another human being with joy and awe. They would smile and wave and maybe blow their horns or pluck their harps in greeting. Even if the person they met was a stranger, even one of another race or nationality or lifestyle, they would show with their greeting that they really believed that the other person had inherent worth and dignity.

FEEDING AND BEING FED

In my mid-50s I became a single adult for the first time, wholly responsible for feeding myself. It was a journey of exploration and discovery. It was a land I had dwelt close to, been surrounded by, all of my life, but now I saw it with new eyes.

One of my discoveries was the joy of feeding people. After some time spent developing the skills necessary to feed myself, I began to actually invite people into my home and serve them food that I had prepared. Not just an entree or appetizer or dessert but a whole meal I had planned, shopped for, chopped, measured, mixed, cooked, and served. And these people, sitting at my table, ate the food I prepared—they took it into their bodies.

I discovered that to do this for someone—to feed them—is to give life. The food gives life, and the person who prepares and serves the food gives life. I was a life-giver.

There were other discoveries: the sensual quality of food preparation, the colors and textures, the surprises of cutting vegetables open and seeing their inner patterns. Oh how I loved bell peppers! I loved the smells that filled the room as things began to braise or simmer or bake.

And I discovered this: The person who receives the gift of the food gives a precious gift as well. It is the gift of trust, an affirmation of the life-giver.

Feeding the body is not all there is to giving life. We who gather in religious community give life, whether or not we have ever sliced a pepper. We transform ordinary entities—a bell, a flame, a touch of a hand, musical notes, a smile, a tear, words, a coffee cup—into spiritual sustenance. We serve it up, and we eat. We are the feeders, and we are those who are fed.

SONGS I SANG

Once upon a time—this goes back to the 1960s—
I used to travel around some and play the banjo and
sing folk songs in front of audiences. Some of the
songs I sang mocked and ridiculed women. There
are many songs like that in the folk tradition, reflect-
ing the fact that sexism has permeated all levels
of our culture for as long as we know. I sang these
songs because I thought they were funny. A couple of
them made fun of women who were fat or ugly. One
made fun of a woman who was so eager to please a
man that she would do almost anything. The worst
one of all went like this:

> It's a shame to whip your wife on Sunday.
> It's a shame to whip your wife on Sunday.
> When you've got Monday, Tuesday, Wednesday,
>   Thursday, Friday, Saturday,
> It's a shame to whip your wife on Sunday.

In those years, I sang that song dozens of times,
and the audiences laughed and applauded.

In 1973, I sang at a meeting in Ann Arbor, Michi-
gan. I included that song and some of the others.
My audience laughed and applauded. Afterward, a
woman came up to me. She didn't look angry; she
wasn't scolding. She simply said, "I wish you wouldn't
sing songs that belittle women."

I can't remember how I responded. Maybe I just stood there with my mouth open. I know this: I never sang those songs again.

That woman liberated me; she empowered me. She made it possible for me to change. She did two things. She named what I was doing: singing songs that belittled women. And she told me what she wanted: for me to stop doing it. I can't remember whether I had given any serious thought to the issue before that day. If so, it had made no difference in my behavior. But her words made the difference.

I met her again years later and thanked her for the gift she had given me. She could not remember the incident.

ABUNDANCE

The parsonage had a large back yard, and the back part of it had been left to grow wild for years. A lot of sumac grew there, as well as bittersweet vine and poison ivy.

I didn't go back there very often, but Whiskers-the-Cat, who lived at the parsonage, prowled that wilderness and killed small creatures for sport.

One day, I discovered blackberries in amongst the wild tangle. I made four trips on hot July days, collecting scratches and bites, sighting little snakes, long-leg spiders, and tiny chiggers, to pick the elusive purple-black fruit. The cat accompanied me, stealthily.

I took the berries and smushed them, sweetened them, and boiled them down until they became eight little jars of jam. I gave most of them away.

I loved the taste. It was magnified by the memory of picking the berries in that overgrown, uncultivated setting, and of transforming them in the kitchen. I did not create that taste, but I did get it into a useful and accessible form. I tasted some of it that winter when the berry plants were gray and brittle. Another person tasted it in Florida, and still another in the mountains of Colorado.

Many flowers bloom unseen, and there are many berries that no one picks. There is an abundance in the Creation.

Well, at least the material parts of the Creation. It is less clear about non-material things. Has God been extravagant with justice? Is there an excess of human love in the Creation? I think not, not without our help. But we can do it—I believe it—with the gifts we are given. We can transform the world until justice and love grow among the toxic vines and biting bugs.

TUCKED IN

On a quiet suburban street on a Sunday evening, just as it was getting dark, I saw a car pull into a driveway, and then the silhouette of a man walking from the car to the front door of the house, carrying a sleeping child. The child's head lay on the man's shoulder, his arms and legs dangling like the limbs of a puppet. They went in the door, and my imagination filled in the rest of the story.

I imagined that the family had been on a day trip in the car. During the warm summer day the boy had run, played, jumped, shouted, eaten. On the way home, he had fallen asleep in the back seat.

My mind went back twenty-five years, to a time when I was that Dad, driving home from a picnic and a hike in the mountains, singing songs in the car, at last seeing the familiar neighborhood in the car lights, pulling into our driveway, and finding one or more of the kids sleeping so soundly that even carrying them in and dressing them for bed did not disturb their slumber.

And then my mind went back fifty years, to when I was that boy, and I remembered how safe I felt in the darkening back seat, with my parents up front. I could put my head down and doze off, trusting that nothing bad would happen. And I would wake up in bed, thinking, "How did I get here? The last thing I remember is being in the back seat of the car." And I realized that my parents had carried me from the car, put me to bed, and tucked me in.

The early Universalists believed that the fate of a human being was like that. No matter how rough the trip might have been or how badly you might have behaved, at the end you would come home, and it would be a place of trust, safety, and love. Two centuries ago, many people were amazed to hear this message, because most churches told them that at the end of their journey they were more likely to face punishment for all their failings.

So is the Ultimate Truth that our souls will be taken care of in the way a loving parent takes care of a child? I don't know. Certainly much of life is not like that. I was lucky. Many children do not have happy homecomings.

I have no answers for Ultimate Questions, but I do have some Partial Truths that I'm quite sure of. Here is one: There is love in this world. There is trust, and there are places of safety where a person can lay down his or her head for a while. The world is not entirely so, but I'm absolutely certain that the world is partially a place of love. And wherever that love comes from, it is manifested in this world by human beings. We are the agents of that love.

LET ME TELL YOU ABOUT MY GRANDDAUGHTER

I just didn't realize how it was going to be, being a grandparent. I remember all the times people have told me about their grandchildren and I reacted with awe and admiration, but I didn't really understand until now. I've heard that old saw so many times about how the joys of grandparenting are derived from the ability to hand her back to her parents when she begins to cry or needs changing. Well, sometimes that's true. But it points to a greater truth that I prefer to state this way: There's a *purity* about my love for Emma that was not there when my kids were infants.

My love for Emma is not mixed up with a lot of problem solving. Nor is her presence in my life accompanied by losses, like the loss of freedom to go out for the evening. I love Emma just for being, and for being in a relationship with me. Just because she is here in the world, and I'm connected with her, she is a unique, miraculous, mysterious, precious gift.

Emma can't do very much yet. Besides the essential bodily functions, she can make noises and various facial expressions, including the beginnings of a smile, and she can look me in the eye. She can move her arms and feet around, and hold my finger. She has wondrous potential; think of the things she might do with her mind and hands and heart. But

I don't love her for her potential. I love her for who she is right now.

If there's a hierarchy of loving relationships, I'd have to affirm first the ones that require great sacrifice. I'd let parents have the front seats on the bus to paradise. After all, if it weren't for parents, there wouldn't be any grandparents. And anyway, I'm already in paradise when I'm with Emma.

ON BUYING A CEMETERY PLOT

I am a world-class procrastinator. I tend to do things at the very last minute, just before disaster strikes. But once, to my everlasting credit, I did something ahead of time. I purchased a cemetery plot.

I tried to examine my motives for buying this plot. None of my family was pressuring me to do it. I've got plenty of other things to do with my money and my time.

One motive is a desire to be remembered. I like the idea of my great-grandchildren stopping by to see my name on a marker. And I like it that future members of that beautiful church you can see through the trees might notice on the marker that I was the minister there a long time ago.

Is this vanity? Yeah. But it's my vanity. And it's an orderly and traditional kind of vanity. So to heck with it, I bought the plot.

There is a usefulness to cemeteries that goes beyond remembering those who have died. Cemeteries help us acknowledge and accept our limits. Maybe that's why we often find them located next to churches—so that one can look out from the sanctuary, the safe place, and see the grave markers.

Until we can live in the presence of death, we will not know the value of life—we will not be fully grateful for the gift of life, and will not be prepared to make full use of this gift to enjoy and serve the Creation.

Perhaps this is the ultimate spiritual paradox: It is the finitude of life that makes it possible for life to reveal something of eternity. It is mortality that connects us with the transcendent.

A GRAY WHALE AND HER CALF IN THE
LAGUNA SAN IGNACIO

Come, little one, I will take you to meet the humans,
the creatures that skim about on the surface,
living in the air, supported by their noisy boats.
It is important for you to know about them.

The humans here are our friends.
They will not hurt you.
Other humans, whom we may meet
on our long journey northward,
will try to kill you, and me,
and the other members of our pod.
But these humans are our friends.

Here is one of their boats. Hear the voices?
There are young ones in this boat who are eager
    to see us.
Hear them squeal with delight.
Put your head above the water and see them.
Swim next to me under the boat
and look at them from the other side.

The elders teach that the humans come
hoping to learn from us, to learn
about the preservation of the earth.
I am not sure of this, but if there is
even a small chance that it is true,
then we must impart this wisdom.

It is not done with language, for we do not speak
their language. It is done simply by looking
into their eyes, and they into ours, and by touching.

Come now, next to me,
and rise next to the humans' boat,
so they may touch us. There. It is done.

Acknowledgments

Thank you, friends, who read all or parts of this work and gave me encouragement, straight talk and helpful advice about it. First, my wife and most important critic and encourager, Kitty Ward. And Deb Cayer, Dan King, Ken Read-Brown, Carol Rosine, and Karen Kettlety.

Thanks to colleagues who early on showed me some of the possibilities of the short essay, especially the late Clarke Dewey Wells.

Thanks to poet and professor Tom Whitbread, for advice and encouragement given long ago.

And thanks to these talented, supportive, challenging editors at Skinner House: Mary Benard and Marshall Hawkins.

Unitarians and Universalists have been publishing prayer collections and meditation manuals for more than 160 years. In 1841 the Unitarians broke with their tradition of addressing only theological topics and published *Short Prayers for the Morning and Evening of Every Day in the Week, with Occasional Prayers and Thanksgivings.* Over the years, the Unitarians published many more volumes of prayers, including Theodore Parker's selections. In 1938 *Gaining a Radiant Faith* by Henry H. Saunderson launched the tradition of an annual Lenten manual.

Several Universalist collections appeared in the early nineteenth century. A comprehensive *Book of Prayers* was published in 1839, featuring both public and private devotions. Like the Unitarians, the Universalists published Lenten manuals, and in the 1950s they complemented this series with Advent manuals.

Since 1961, the year the Unitarians and Universalists consolidated, the Lenten manual has evolved into a meditation manual.

2009	*With or Without Candlelight* Victoria Safford, Editor
2008	*Sonata for Voice and Silence* Mark Belletini
2007	*Amethyst Beach* Barbara Merritt
2006	*A Guest of the World* Jeffrey Lockwood
2005	*For All That Is Our Life* Helen and Eugene Pickett, Editors

Admire the Moon Mary Wellemeyer

2004 *We Build Temples in the Heart* Patrick Murfin
Consider the Lilies Stephen M. Shick

2003 *Walking Toward Morning* Victoria Safford
How We Are Called Mary Benard and
Kirstie Anderson, Editors

2002 *Instructions in Joy* Nancy Shaffer
Roller-skating as a Spiritual Discipline
Christopher Buice

2001 *This Piece of Eden* Vanessa Rush Southern
Dancing in the Empty Spaces David O. Rankin

2000 *Glad to Be Human* Kaaren Anderson
Out of the Ordinary Gordon B. McKeeman

1999 *The Rock of Ages at the Taj Mahal* Meg Barnhouse
Morning Watch Barbara Pescan

1998 *Glory, Hallelujah! Now Please Pick Up Your Socks*
Jane Ellen Mauldin
Evening Tide Elizabeth Tarbox

1997 *A Temporary State of Grace* David S. Blanchard
Green Mountain Spring and Other Leaps of Faith
Gary A. Kowalski

1996 *Taking Pictures of God* Bruce T. Marshall
Blessing the Bread Lynn Ungar

1995 *In the Holy Quiet of This Hour* Richard S. Gilbert

1994 *In the Simple Morning Light* Barbara Rohde

1993 *Life Tides* Elizabeth Tarbox
The Gospel of Universalism Tom Owen-Towle

1992 *Noisy Stones* Robert Walsh

1991 *Been in the Storm So Long* Mark Morrison-Reed
and Jacqui James, Editors

1990 *Into the Wilderness* Sara Moores Campbell

1989 *A Small Heaven* Jane Ranney Rzepka

1988	*The Numbering of Our Days* Anthony Friess Perrino
1987	*Exaltation* David B. Parke, Editor
1986	*Quest* Kathy Fuson Hurt
1985	*The Gift of the Ordinary* Charles S. Stephen, Jr., Editor
1984	*To Meet the Asking Years* Gordon B. McKeeman, Editor
1983	*Tree and Jubilee* Greta W. Crosby
1981	*Outstretched Wings of the Spirit* Donald S. Harrington
1980	*Longing of the Heart* Paul N. Carnes
1979	*Portraits from the Cross* David Rankin
1978	*Songs of Simple Thanksgiving* Kenneth L. Patton
1977	*Promise of Spring* Clinton Lee Scott
1976	*The Strangeness of This Business* Clarke D. Wells
1975	*In Unbroken Line* Chris Raible, Editor
1974	*Stopping Places* Mary Lou Thompson
1973	*The Tides of Spring* Charles W. Grady
1972	*73 Voices* Chris Raible and Ed Darling, Editors
1971	*Bhakti, Santi, Love, Peace* Jacob Trapp
1970	*Beginning Now* J. Donald Johnston
1969	*Answers in the Wind* Charles W. McGehee
1968	*The Trying Out* Richard Kellaway
1967	*Moments of a Springtime* Rudolf W. Nemser
1966	*Across the Abyss* Walter D. Kring
1965	*The Sound of Silence* Raymond Baughan
1964	*Impassioned Clay* Ralph Helverson
1963	*Seasons of the Soul* Robert T. Weston
1962	*The Uncarven Image* Phillip Hewett
1961	*Parts and Proportions* Arthur Graham